Expanding PERSPECTIVES OF THE HEART

BRIAN ROSCOE

EXPANDING PERSPECTIVES OF THE HEART
COPYRIGHT © 2021 BY BRIAN ROSCOE

All rights reserved. No part of this publication may be reproduced, distributed, or transmitted in any form or by any means, including photocopying, recording, or other electronic or mechanical methods, without the prior written permission of the author, except in the case of brief quotations embodied in critical reviews and certain other noncommercial uses permitted by copyright law.

The content of this book is for general informational purposes only. It is not meant to be used, nor should it be used, to diagnose or treat any medical condition or to replace the services of your physician or other healthcare provider. The advice and strategies contained in the book may not be suitable for all readers.

Neither the author, publisher, nor any of their employees or representatives guarantees the accuracy of information in this book or its usefulness to a particular reader, nor are they responsible for any damage or negative consequence that may result from any treatment, action taken, or inaction by any person reading or following the information in this book.

For permission requests or to contact the author, visit:
brianroscoeauthor.com

ISBN-13: 978-1-957348-11-7

PRINTED IN THE UNITED STATES OF AMERICA

Expanding PERSPECTIVES OF THE HEART

*"Whatever we are waiting for—peace of mind,
contentment, grace, the inner awareness of
simple abundance—it will surely come to us,
but only when we are ready to receive it
with an open and grateful heart."*
-Sarah Ban Breathnach

There are times in our lives when we have to open our heart to the transformation that comes from answering the question: "Who am I now?" With all the changes in my life, having experienced all the difficulties and the joys, the lessons learned and the missed opportunities, "Who am I now?" We need to open to new paradigms of seeing ourselves, so much so that it rocks the very core of what we previously used as our identity. And then we ask the question, using the answers and the question itself, to find and remember an essence denied, some quality of love forgotten, a remembering of a truth within ourselves ready to be seen again.

So let's heal this life! Let's come back to ourselves! Let's remember the deepest truth within ourselves rather than getting sidetracked by all the gutter and inner distractions constantly thrown at us. Let's remember who we are. Let's dedicate our lives to remembering the very heart of who we are.

There is a question that we need to ask ourselves, especially when we're stuck in our judgment, anger, or any other type of dark mental obsessions: Does this thought or can this action, which originated from my thinking, enhance, add to, help, or empower our common humanity in any way? Does this truly benefit anyone, or is there a better way for me to see this situation?

Expanding PERSPECTIVES OF THE HEART

"Love and compassion are necessities, not luxuries. Without them, humanity cannot survive."
-Dalai Lama

JOURNEY PROMPT
EXERCISE: **"I'm open to seeing that."**

When you're stuck in difficulty, and even when you're not, create a habit of asking yourself, for the sake of yourself: "Is there a better, stronger, kinder, more compassionate way for me to participate in my life? I'm open to seeing that."

Writing or journaling helps us uncover and explore the truths hidden in our heart. It also helps us expose the lies and belief systems trapped in our minds—concepts and ideas that we've adopted into our lives and convinced ourselves to be true. Knowing the difference between the two, truth and contrived belief, is what allows us our *freedom*.

JOURNEY PROMPT

Spend ten, twenty, even thirty minutes a day journaling about absolutely anything. Explore the truth of your beliefs, the questions about what the world has taught you. Free your mind, unleash your heart, and let whatever wants to flow onto that piece of paper exuberantly erupt forward into your world! Answers won't come forward unless questions are somehow asked. So, ask, and listen for your truth.

Expanding PERSPECTIVES OF THE HEART

Only the *finest of Thread* separates any of us from another.

It's not always easy remembering that we're all the same, and all absolutely precious in our creation. But maybe it wasn't meant to be easy, and as hard as it is to remember our common ties, it's in the journey of remembering it that helps us find peace with each other.

JOURNEY PROMPT

If you ever find yourself stuck in a quality of thinking that keeps you from experiencing the beauty in someone, someone who's different from you or has different ways than you, allow yourself the space to start again with them. Imagine something new, something different for yourself and for that other person. There is a freedom in beginning again whenever you feel stuck, away from your love.

"The little space within the heart is as great as the vast universe. The heavens and the earth are there, and the sun and the moon and the stars. Fire and lightning and winds are there, and all that now is and all that is not."
-*The Upanishads*

The outside crust of a person is no indication of what lays within. Hold your judgment until you can see through the eyes of your heart.

Expanding PERSPECTIVES OF THE HEART

JOURNEY PROMPT

Have you ever formed an opinion about someone only to find out later that they didn't fit your judgment? Our judgment works in many directions. Someone who looks perfect turns out to be internally rough and struggling, or just plain mean. And someone who really looks harsh on the outside, who you judge to be difficult or scary or, again, just plain mean, turns out to be truly human in a way you rarely see or meet.

Our judgments are destined to be wrong. They're based on assumptions, and in our assumptions, we don't know anything for sure. This is where we have to step up to the plate and find out the truth of the situation with integrity. If we can't do that then what we're thinking is just none of our business! And we're in charge of making it so.

The concept of free will dictates that we choose the quality of thought that we walk through life with. Rather than negativity and fear, we can choose to be vessels of compassion, kindness, and love, and we can be present to those qualities and allow them to flow through us, guiding our lives.

It's easy to get distracted from the fact that we, indeed, choose our thinking. We tend to slip into believing that our circumstances and dramas choose our thought. It takes a true moment of strength to realize and admit when we've chosen to negatively attach to a false or exaggerated story about something that never should have been given importance in our world. The truth of your life is that you're the author, and you just need to start writing what you know, and what you *really* know is love. So, let your mind and your heart start working together again. There's a whole lot of editing to do!

Expanding PERSPECTIVES OF THE HEART

JOURNEY PROMPT

What does it look like to see yourself as love and not fear, compassion instead of anger?

Who do you become when you reject the story of fearful thinking and embrace the truth, the gentler strength of love?

Who are you then? It's worth working on.

We are all the same. Deep down inside, governed by our hearts, we all know it. Fear makes us think we're different, it can make us feel separated and estranged from one another, but fear is a poor master to guide your life by, and beyond it, we are all connected through our hearts.

At our best, we relentlessly search for a stronger love in our lives. We explore new, more compassionate ways of being that keep us pointed towards what we know to be true. In that, we change, and our very neurology shifts to adapt to a life centered in the heart.

This journey is the ultimate full contact sport! In a very real way, we are choosing to use our gift of free will and free thought to reinforce new energetic patterns that point us toward peace—peace for ourselves and for all that we share the world with. The very cells in our bodies will alter themselves to accommodate a more

Expanding PERSPECTIVES OF THE HEART

complete and full personal transformation. You not only change your thinking in this journey, you recreate your form.

You. You already know your purpose. Listen to the whisper, already a part of you, constantly reminding you who you are. Listen for the quiet voice that inspires, *"Grow and keep growing. Expand your love into everything that you think and all that you are."*

JOURNEY PROMPT

Keeping in mind that we all have our own way of dancing to the music within. Answer the question: what might your dance look like? And then spend your life celebrating your amazing self!

It's hard to see how beautiful life is when we're stuck trying to fix something that doesn't need to be fixed; something that just needs to be left alone and may actually be *perfect as it is*.

Expanding PERSPECTIVES OF THE HEART

JOURNEY PROMPT

Take a moment to meditate on the phrase above. How does this apply to the hustle and bustle of the day?

Ask yourself periodically, "Am I being a perfectionist or overly critical about something or some part of my life that is really just fine and flowing just as it needs to?"

Can you apply this phrase to your life more often? "Everything is just as it should be."

> *"The world is full of magic things,*
> *patiently waiting for our senses to grow sharper."*
> *-W.B. Yeats*

No matter what you think a challenge looks like in the moment, you always have the opportunity to embrace it with more grace and healthier strength.

I mean, you've got to have a goal! Work on embracing life with grace, no matter what's unfolding in front of you, because fear just isn't usually very productive. Trying to infuse a little grace into a situation is just healthier, and it definitely feels better and brings out the best in you. And in the long run, it's a far stronger approach to life… totally worth the effort.

Expanding PERSPECTIVES OF THE HEART

JOURNEY PROMPT

The potential to see the situations of our lives through new and different lenses is an acquired talent that we need to work and strive for. It doesn't come easy to us in this world because we tend to get caught up in needing to be right about whatever thinking we've attached to. But when we can open up to imagining something different, it helps us become more responsible for our own peace and assists us in exploring our internal world for the higher truth of any particular situation. To see life through lenses that help us walk forward with more love, strength, and openness is essential to our wellbeing and the wellbeing of those we interact with. It's worth the stretch.

> *"With everything that has happened to you, you can either feel sorry for yourself or treat what has happened as a gift. Everything is either an opportunity to grow or an obstacle to keep you from growing. You get to choose."*
> -Wayne W. Dyer

When we're not mindful of our thinking, many of our choices concerning life and how we behave in it can seem to get made automatically, almost like we're on autopilot. It happens even with the important choices, the ones that could clearly use some fresh thought around them. We decide things in life based out of habit. Perhaps they're automatic because we make them from a perspective of fear, or we decide not to choose something simply because we're unfamiliar with it. We live our lives reflexively, avoiding the new, the different or confusing, or labeling it as wrong. We may even make choices that can dramatically impact our lives out of just plain laziness, not wanting to make more work for ourselves than we have to by choosing something new and unknown.

We forget that we always have permission to explore new ways of thinking and behaving, ways that work better for us or just feel better and resonate more with our hearts. When we choose to, we can see anything through fresh eyes, view any situation or judgment differently, no matter what we're confronted with or what's happening around us.

JOURNEY PROMPT

In all ways, open yourself and your heart to that place of love that you have not previously recognized, because it's the biggest part of who you are.

How can we possibly know what direction the cascade of life's dominoes would have fallen if things had not happened just exactly the way they did?

Bless whatever is and its yet unknown purpose.

Expanding PERSPECTIVES OF THE HEART

JOURNEY PROMPT

Make a list of situations that turned out fine, even when you were tempted to micromanage and control them. Was it better or worse for the final outcome that you didn't have full control over everything that occurred? Can you be sure?

1)

2)

3)

"The moment you have in your heart this extraordinary thing called love and feel the depth, the delight, the ecstasy of it, you will discover that for you the world is transformed."
-Jiddu Krishnamurti

ACTUALLY, THE BALL IS ALWAYS IN OUR COURT!

We all get caught up in negative thinking from time to time, probably way more than we'd like. Stepping past our ego or shame and admitting that we're stuck is the most important part of turning ourselves around. In the acknowledgment that we're stuck in negative, toxic thinking and ill will, we automatically and very naturally open ourselves to finding an antidote to that thought. This helps us shift our intention and creates new, healthier, and more compassionate ways of being, because we are willing to own our misstep and open up to something different, something stronger.

Expanding PERSPECTIVES OF THE HEART

Food and thinking choices have a kind of parallel existence in our mind. It can suddenly occur to us that we're eating unhealthy, rancid, or just plain poisonous food. It's in this moment that we can choose to continue or stop, to participate in getting sick or to protect our health. Why would we willingly, stubbornly continue to participate in a harmful and toxic activity? Yet we stubbornly continue to consume food and thoughts out of addiction and habit. Is this what we were taught? Do we do this because it's the way we've always done it, or because we just don't want to try anything different? Whatever the answer, it's what we know—until we know better, until we come to our senses. Our job is to find that better way.

JOURNEY PROMPT

Whether it be your thinking choices or your food choices, take the time to open to new thought. Work out an *antidote thought*—a process of creating thought choices that manifest health rather than languishing in the rancidity of previous ways.

Expanding PERSPECTIVES OF THE HEART

Life is a mysterious culmination of events, continuously unfolding with a depth of purpose and intention we can never grasp the full magnitude of.

> "If you can look into the seeds of time and say, 'Which grain will grow, and which will not?' speak then to me"
> -William Shakespeare, *Macbeth*

JOURNEY PROMPT

Trust that life is unfolding perfectly as it's meant to, that our lessons and growth are in good hands, and your only job is to be present with it, helping the lessons of life guide us forward, molding us into our truth, our strength and our love.

"We can learn to see each other and see ourselves in each other, and recognize that human beings are more alike than we are unalike."
-Maya Angelou

You choose what path you walk in life, in your relationships, and in how you love. Only you. With personal integrity, choose where, how, and why you walk in your journey. Live life from the strength of your heart, through a clarity of a mind uncomplicated by fear, with a love that lives through you in words and deeds, and with humor by your side. Life is way too short to leave out the humor!

Expanding PERSPECTIVES OF THE HEART

JOURNEY PROMPT

I can live and love with more strength, clarity, and humor by letting go of these [behaviors, habits, attitudes] in my very human journey:

-
-
-

I can live and love with more strength, clarity, and humor by including these [behaviors, habits, attitudes] in my very human journey:

-
-
-

(Warning! Additional room or journaling may be required!)

MUDITA: ANTIDOTE FOR ENVY AND JEALOUSY

> *"It's not what you look at that matters,
> it's what you see."*
> *–Henry David Thoreau*

Mudita is a Sanskrit word that means unselfish joy, being happy about the joys that other beings feel, or joy in the good fortune of others. Its opposite would be similar to envy or jealousy.

There's a pleasure that comes from finding joy in other people's wellbeing. An example might be the feelings experienced by a parent

Expanding PERSPECTIVES OF THE HEART

watching their child take their first step, or taking pleasure in an older child's success and accomplishments.

Mudita is not exactly pride because the only concern is for the other. Mudita is a pure joy. There's no direct payoff financially or emotionally for the participant. There's only interest for the wellbeing of the other.

JOURNEY PROMPT

What a beautiful way to live your life and a wonderful quality to bring into your interaction with others! Mudita is way better than envy and jealousy, both of which slowly poison you and fool you into thinking they're maintaining you in your strength. That's the sneaky little trick of judgment.

> *"For small creatures such as we,
> the vastness is bearable
> only through love."*
> *–Carl Sagan*

Often, the way we react to life's events is born more out of habitual behavior than choice. That fast, often unthoughtful reaction, where we jump to conclusions and create trouble for ourselves, evolved as part of our personality to keep us safe from potential hazards. It's a mechanism created for self-preservation, acquired from countless generations of programmed and socially expectable behavior. We grow up believing that this learned, automatically reactive behavior keeps us safe and protects our chosen groups.

There's a mistake here. We believe that our experience needs to be defined as "unsafe," and that fear and reaction are our best tools to counter our feelings of vulnerability. However, when we allow ourselves to mindfully feel and be in that vulnerability, it gives us a more neutral place to choose from. We give ourselves an opportunity to see things differently. We pause long enough to determine how we want to participate in life, to find our healthiest of responses, and to ask the necessary questions:

- Am I actually safe here?
- How do I step forward from here in peace?
- What is my best choice here?
- How can love guide this moment?

JOURNEY PROMPT

Pick a familiar situation that you typically find yourself reacting to and use these questions to reframe where you typically go with that particular circumstance:

- Seriously, what's the truth of it? Am I actually safe in this situation?
- How can I step forward from here in a more peaceful way?
- Is there a better choice for me to make here compared to the choices I've made in the past?
- How can I encourage love to better guide this moment?

Expanding PERSPECTIVES OF THE HEART

> *"Make a gift of your life and lift all mankind by being kind, considerate, forgiving, and compassionate at all times, in all places, and under all conditions with everyone as well as yourself. This is the greatest gift anyone can give."*
> –David R. Hawkins

We all try to relate to one another through the lenses we develop through our past experiences, both enjoyable as well as difficult. These old, often cloudy and misinformed lenses can limit us, and they can easily impact the way we view our world. It's important for us to put some effort into cultivating newer, cleaner lenses to look through and move into life with. Perhaps we refocus and adjust our lens so we can see the events of our lives in a more humble, kinder way, or we re-work our looking glass into a more rational, less reactive lens—to look through a life lens that helps us see our world through something more loving, one that allows us to, for example, be a good listener, or to have greater compassion and kindness for ourselves as well as others. Ultimately, the goal is for us to find that internal spot where we can live more clearly in our wisdom, in our truth, and focused in our ability to function more and more through our hearts.

Expanding PERSPECTIVES OF THE HEART

JOURNEY PROMPT

Old lenses:

1.

2.

3.

New, more preferable lenses:

1.

2.

3.

Okay, now *smile* into the new ones!

KEEP IT SIMPLE!

At the 2011 Three Principles Convention in London, I listened to Linda Pransky as she explained a visit that she once had with Sydney Banks.

Apparently, at the time, Linda and her husband, George, felt like they were at the end of their marriage. They couldn't get along, couldn't talk nicely to each other or agree on anything. They could barely stand one another's company and spent most of their time arguing and wondering why they were bothering to be in a relationship at all… not an uncommon scenario for any of us.

So, as it went, Linda and George related their

concerns to Syd. They spent a significant amount of time explaining what was wrong while Syd listened on, until he posed a question to the both of them.

Syd asked if they could remember a time when things were better—a time when they enjoyed themselves and relished in their time spent together. It wasn't long before they were enthralled in the memories of how wonderful things had been, remembering how they had stayed up till the wee hours of the morning, talking and laughing; how spending time together was the primary thing they wanted to do, and how they just beamed when they saw one another and felt so totally connected. I believe Linda said that Syd just looked at them and said, "Well, do more of that."

In other words, you're responsible for what you bring into the room—no one can make that choice for you—so bring something good.

JOURNEY PROMPT

Make your list of forgotten joys and neglected interests. Find some things you love to do, things and activities that bring you joy, peace, happiness, some way of being that you've forgotten about or haven't done in a while, and make a list:

1)

2)

3)

Now, do that more.

Expanding PERSPECTIVES OF THE HEART

OWNING WHO YOU ARE

"You must find the place inside yourself where nothing is impossible."
-Deepak K. Chopra

Hmm, I thought it would be easier than this, but what else can I do? On my journey, I am a fish in water. *I cannot resist swimming, so I swim, and sometimes, I swim well.*

"The journey from teaching about love to allowing myself to be loved proved much longer than I realized."
-Henri Nouwen

JOURNEY PROMPT

Patience. Patience with the journey. But it's not like we have a choice! Being patient is one of the biggest lessons we have, it's a huge requirement in this journey. How odd it is that we get immersed in a journey that requires patience. There's a prankster out there that calls itself the creator, and guaranteed, just when you think you're doing great, life implodes a little—the basement floods, or the car breaks down, a check bounces, someone leaves, someone dies—the point being, there's no part of the journey that has a beginning and an end that doesn't require a whole lot of work from and through us, and that does, indeed, require patience. As a matter of fact, the biggest issue is often believing that we can whiz through life without effort, or that we're ever done working through any of our "stuff."

Saying that I don't make choices based out of fear would definitely be disingenuous. I do. I don't like it, but I defiantly catch myself doing it.

Like everyone else, I make fear-choices, and it's often without ever knowing it until I can find the space to pause, look back at myself, and see that I've gone there again and that it's time to correct the course of my ship again!

However, because of my choice to correct, I know, in the depth of who I am, that my intention is to walk with more love and preferably without fear. There's a comfort and a confidence knowing this about myself, knowing that my ultimate desire is to know love in a deeper way, and to have it flow through my life, all my life.

JOURNEY PROMPT

What choice would I make if fear was not a factor in this moment? What would I do in the absence of fear?

Take a minute and try to identify any quality of fear that directs your choices in life. Now, imagine what it would feel like for that fear to be absent from your consciousness. How might that change your choice in that moment? In other words, who are you in the absence of your fear? What does it feel like? What does it look like? When we can open ourselves to these questions, it's only then that the answers make themselves available. We must look at ourselves, look at the qualities of thought we participate in life with, and be open to acknowledging our fear so that we may willfully step beyond it.

Expanding PERSPECTIVES OF THE HEART

"Life is a luminous pause between two great
mysteries which themselves are one."
-Carl Jung

**The world is a *miracle*,
so don't be surprised when
you see one. Expect it!**

JOURNEY PROMPT

The truest work of life helps us cultivate the understanding that we're never really stuck, either in our thought or our circumstances, because neither one of these defines the quality of our experience. No matter what, we're okay. We have the amazing capacity to always think again, always imagine something new. It puts the quality of our experience in our own hands, because life can always be seen and experienced from a stronger, even gentler perspective than could ever be available through our fear or our anguish and suffering. There's always room to see a lesson, find a truth in every situation.

Sometimes I get the feeling this planet acts as a medium for us to develop in, meant to inspire growth and push us toward more love. And as far as our growth is concerned, it seems like the ball is always in our court, and we always have the power to make our world whatever we want it to become.

Expanding PERSPECTIVES OF THE HEART

> *"Nobody has ever measured, not even poets,
> how much the heart can hold."*
> *-Zelda Fitzgerald*

**Eagerly accept the *gift*.
It awaits only your recognition.**

JOURNEY PROMPT

So often, we're surprised when something fancy happens to us—a synchronistic experience, a perceived miracle, a sense of forgiveness unexpected, a beautiful event in our presence. But we forget that we live in a world of infinite creation, so, of course, the *fantastically amazing* occurs. We live in and through a world and life experience that's without any doubt *fantastically amazing*! So, have at it, friend! This is our chance to be part of the show, so show up already, and stand in awe of what has been given to you and everyone!

Expanding PERSPECTIVES OF THE HEART

A WARRIOR'S CHALLENGE

The compulsive over-thinker. It's not hard to become one. As a matter of fact, we have a tendency to attract it to ourselves, as though, somehow, it makes us feel like we're accomplishing something.

We're all vulnerable to our compulsive thinking tendencies, becoming almost addicted to relentlessly churning ourselves through our thoughts. Walking back and forth through our assumptions, perceptions, and the personalized happenings of our lives.

We all get wrapped up in our thought, trying to

figure our way past the confusion, the quandaries and challenges that come with being human. Habitually falling into the idea that if we put enough jaw clenching effort into an issue, our stress and worry can make the difference, we fool ourselves into believing we can "intellect" ourselves out of anything. But we need to learn to step back from all that, because, for the most part, we're not going to "think" our way out of our suffering, contemplate our way out of our pain, and our mental machinery is not going to grind its way out of whatever struggle we're entertaining in the moment. In truth, it's in our ability to let go of our intellectual processing that we're able to find our front row ticket into our answer machine. That's where the gold is, in releasing. It's what allows us to open up to all the new thought and previously unavailable solutions that we're really looking for. This is what allows thought to emerge from a place of inspiration rather than through our anxiety. Whether it's a huge issue or a mild upset, when we can set our incessant thinking about something off to the side, even for a moment, we create opportunities for fresh thought for ourselves. We open ourselves to an internal glimpse of inspired thinking that often presents very unexpected solutions to our struggles. You just may never find those lost car keys until you stop looking for them. Your higher power knows all, but it's shy and just needs a little silence before it speaks.

When you're stuck in a difficult place, how do you tend get yourself out of it? What might it feel like to let go of your thinking around a problem? If you have no extraction plans, heres a hint: Put some distance between yourself and your problem and consider the event that you're tangled up in. What does it look like from a more neutral standpoint? Ask your stuck self, is this productive? Is it important? Is it in everyone's higher interest to release this problem, open it up into a different framework of thought? Can something positive like gratitude or some quality of grace be integrated into this situation? So often, we do this naturally, without prompting.

Losing something only to remember where we put it when we started doing something else, or hearing the whisper of forgiveness and understanding when we decide to read a book to take our mind off that bitch, bastard, brat kid, or idiot boss, who we would really just want

Expanding PERSPECTIVES OF THE HEART

to be able to love. So when stuck in thinking about life's challenges and traumas, get in touch with your healthy distraction, learn the art of doing something else so a little grace can wiggle through—and while you're at it, if you can, try to make it something fun!

> Be the vehicle of your own *happiness*, and the driver, too!
> After all, who else would you
> give your keys to?

> It's as though we all have our own
> personal chauffeur called "Us,"
> asking, "What direction would
> your mind like to go today?"

> And *we choose the quality
> of our thinking*, and
> thus the direction we take our heart.

> *"We are made to persist. That's how we find out who we are."*
> *−Tobias Wolff*

www.ingramcontent.com/pod-product-compliance
Lightning Source LLC
Chambersburg PA
CBHW021432070526
44577CB00001B/169

* 9 7 8 1 9 5 7 3 4 8 1 1 7 *